MAX BECKMANN

THE SELF-PORTRAITS

BY PETER SELZ

Afterword by Nathan Oliveira

GAGOSIAN GALLERY

RIZZOLI
NEW YORK

First published in the United States of America
in 1992 by Rizzoli International Publications, Inc.,
300 Park Avenue South, New York, NY 10010,
in association with Gagosian Gallery
980 Madison Avenue, New York, NY 10021.

Library of Congress Cataloging-in-Publication Data:
Selz, Peter Howard, 1919-
    Max Beckmann: the self-portraits/Peter Selz:
    afterword by Nathan Oliveira.
    p.   cm.
    Includes bibliographical references and index.
    ISBN 0-8478-1640-0
    1. Beckmann, Max, 1884-1950—Self-portraits.
    2. Beckmann, Max, 1884-1950—Criticism and
    interpretation. I. Beckmann, Max, 1884-1950.
    II. Gagosian Gallery. III. Title.
    ND1329.B4S4   1992
    759.3—dc20   92-20061
                                                CIP

This volume is the fourth in a series of
Gagosian Gallery/Rizzoli, New York publications.

Series Editor: Raymond Foye
Editors: Andrea Codrington and Don Kennison
Production director: Elizabeth White
Gagosian Gallery project coordinators:
Jessica Fredericks and Robert Pincus-Witten

Design and typesetting:
Step Graphics Inc., New York

Acknowledgments:
Grateful acknowledgment is made to the lenders to
the exhibition, and to Maya Beckmann,
Mayen Wuerdig-Beckmann, and Dr. Dietmar Elger,
Sprengel Museum, Hannover.

Frontis Image:
Max Beckmann in St. Louis, November 1949
Courtesy, Private Collection.

Printed and bound in Italy

CONTENTS

Self-Portrait with Greenish Background. 1912
Oil on canvas, 18 x 17" (46 x 43.5 cm)
Private Collection.
Göpel 154

and was taken on by one of the most exclusive galleries in Germany. At the precocious age of 29 Beckmann had his first retrospective exhibition in Berlin, which was accompanied by a monograph.

During this period he painted the very tender *Double Portrait Max Beckmann and Minna Beckmann-Tube* (1909), a very private depiction of the artist and his young bride leaning against each other and looking out at the world with dreamy but melancholy expressions. Three years later he returned to the looser brushwork of the Florence picture, and depicts himself with a reserved, taciturn, almost alienated mien in *Self-Portrait with Greenish Background*. In a drypoint etching made just before the outbreak of the war, the artist appears with a more intense and determined look, confronting the viewer with resolute confidence.

Beckmann did not share the general enthusiasm that greeted the declaration of war in July 1914. In fact he told his wife, "I will not shoot at the French. I've learned too much from them. And at the Russians neither. Dostoevsky is my friend."[7] Choosing alternate service, the

Self-Portrait. 1914
Drypoint, plate: 9⅜ x 6⅞" (24 x 17.5 cm)
Collection, The Brooklyn Museum, by exchange.
Hofmaier 74.

Following pages:
Self-Portrait as Medical Orderly. 1915
Oil on canvas, 21¾ x 15" (55.5 x 38.5 cm)
Collection, Von der Heydt-Museum, Wuppertal.
Göpel 187

The Smoker. 1916
Drypoint, 7 x 5" (17.5 x 12.5 cm)
Collection, Allan Frumkin.
Hofmaier 98

artist volunteered for the medical corps, serving first on the Eastern front and then in Belgium. Beckmann would regard his war experiences as formative for his life and art, as another "manifestation of life, like sickness, love or lust....Everywhere I find deep lines of beauty in the suffering and endurance of this terrible fate."[8] Although he was profoundly affected by the agony and suffering around him, his art remained of paramount importance and kept him from falling prey to despair. In October 1914 he wrote to Minna, "I have been drawing—this is what keeps me from death and danger."[9]

A year later, however, Beckmann suffered a nervous breakdown and was sent to Strasbourg, where he painted *Self-Portrait as a Medical Orderly.* He appears apprehensively turning his head to face the viewer in a momentary, arrested motion that reveals his disturbed condition. The only color accent in this somber painting is the Red Cross emblem on the collar of his military tunic. The experience of war and his personal breakdown changed the artist's life. It caused, as he recalled later, a "great injury to his soul," and brought about a highly significant change

Das Rote Haar   Beckmann
                                                 Der Selbst

Self-Portrait. 1917
Pen and ink on cream laid paper, 15½ x 12½", (38.5 x 31.5 cm)
Collection, The Art Institute of Chicago.

Following pages:
Self-Portrait with Red Scarf. 1917
Oil on canvas, 31½ x 23⅝" (80 x 60 cm)
Collection, Württembergische Staatsgalerie, Stuttgart.
Göpel 194

Self-Portrait with Champagne Glass. 1919
Oil on canvas, 37½ x 21¾" (95 x 55.5 cm)
Private Collection.
Göpel 203

in his painting style. A similar disclosure appears in a sensitive *Self-Portrait* drawing of 1917. Here Beckmann clutches his throat, looking down at the ground with slit eyes in an expression of great pain. The drawing was done, as we see in his inscription, "at night, four in the morning." All the finesse evident in his earlier work is now discarded for an intimate rendition of a tortured individual. At about the same time he painted *Self-Portrait with Red Scarf*, which is not so much an intimate self-portrait as it is an outcry against the injustice of the world. Coming as close to Expressionism as he ever did, Beckmann distorts his own anatomy as well as the space he occupies. Everything in the painting is angular and sharp. The flesh of his body is corpselike and creates a contrast to the bright red scarf wrapped around his neck. The body language is abrupt gesture; the position of the arms and the frightened face depict him, in James Burke's words, as "the horror-stricken witness of the apocalypse."[10]

The world to which Beckmann returned when he went to Frankfurt to find a temporary home with his friends, the

The Night. 1918-1919
Oil on canvas, 52⅓ x 60⅔" (133 x 154 cm)
Collection, Kunstsammlung Nordrhein-Westfalen, Düsseldorf.
Göpel 200

Following pages:
The Dream. 1921
Oil on canvas, 72⅗ x 34⅖" (184.5 x 87.5 cm)
Collection, The Saint Louis Art Museum, Bequest of Morton D. May.
Göpel 208

The Evening (Self-Portrait with the Battenbergs) (from the portfolio *Faces*). 1916
Drypoint, 9 x 7" (22.5 x 18 cm)
Private Collection.
Hofmaier 90

Battenbergs, was totally different from the prosperous Berlin he had left only a year earlier. As the war seemed to linger without end, as the number of dead continued to multiply, and as deprivation and hunger prevailed at home, his own condition of anxiety and agitation persisted. When peace finally came and the Republic was proclaimed in November 1918, there appeared a moment of promise, even euphoria, for a better future. But very soon the new state found itself in total turmoil. Foreign occupation, unemployment, and hunger brought about general hopelessness. The bar in which Beckmann raises his glass in *Self-Portrait with Champagne Glass* is a narrow, confining space. This is an uncanny and forlorn celebration, a distorted image from a desperate café society, which reveals the historical reality of impending doom as well as the loneliness of the solitary drinker. The attempt of the Left to continue the Socialist movement was answered by the brutal murder of its leaders Rosa Luxemburg and Karl Liebknecht in January 1919. Countering the utopian slogan of the immediate postwar period, *"Der*

Self-Portrait (from the portfolio *Hell*). 1918-19
Lithograph, 15 x 12" (38 x 30.5 cm)
Collection, Allan Frumkin.
Hofmaier 139

Following pages:
The Family (from the portfolio *Hell*). 1919
Lithograph, 30 x 18⅕" (76.5 x 46.5 cm)
Collection, Allan Frumkin.
Hofmaier 149

Frontal Self Portrait, House Gable in Background. 1918
Drypoint, 12 x 10" (30.5 x 25.5 cm)
Collection, Garner Tullis.
Hofmaier 125

Mensch ist gut" (Man is good), George Grosz commented cynically, *"Der Mensch ist ein Vieh"* (Man is a beast).

Beckmann responded to the monstrous murders with unremitting paintings of horror and tragedy such as *The Night* (1918-19), and *The Dream* (1921), as well as with numerous graphic works. Printmaking was well suited to express the shattering experience of the artist at this time and was to assume a dominant position in his oeuvre. Prints could be executed rapidly and disseminated in the copious new political journals or printed singly and distributed in portfolios. Furthermore, like many of his predecessors in the history of German art, Beckmann's work was principally determined by line. This stress on linear structure also appears in his paintings during the postwar years. It was at that time that he was most attentive to Germany's Gothic masters and the angularity of their form.

The print cycles Beckmann completed during this harrowing period show a chaotic and disparate world. The cities and their

31/75   Beckmann

"Die Familie"   Beckmann

Selbstbildnis 1918 Einziger Druck (Platte zerstört)   Beckmann 18

Large Self-Portrait. 1919
Drypoint, 9¼ x 7¾" (23.5 x 19.5 cm)
Collection, Peter Selz.
Hofmaier 153

people are disassembled by disaster. Each year a new suite came off his press: *Faces* in 1918, *Hell* in 1919, *City Night* in 1920, *The Annual Fair* in 1921, and *Berlin Journey* in 1922. His own image appears in many of these prints. In the earliest, which the artist originally called *World Theater* until the eminent critic Julius Meier-Graefe changed it to *Faces*, Beckmann is seen several times in tightly compressed family groups, or by himself in sharp isolation cut into the copper plate with nervous agitation. In *Hell*, a suite of large-size lithographs, he appears on the title page an anxious and frightened individual whose terror is revealed by his eyes, which seem to dart about, witness to various disturbing events. There is also Beckmann's family, with the image of his disheartened mother-in-law and his son wearing a steel helmet and a mischievous smile as he plays with make-believe hand grenades, while the artist himself points accusingly toward the street.

In 1919 Beckmann created the *Large Self-Portrait* in drypoint. The artist, a cigarette dangling from his mouth, directs his large, piercing eyes at the viewer with a probing and quizzical expression. His

38/75   „Die Straße"   Beckmann

The Way Home. 1919
Lithograph, 29 x 19" (73.5 x 48 cm)
Collection, Allan Frumkin.
Hofmaier 140

Following pages:
Self-Portrait in Bowler Hat. 1921
Drypoint, printed in black-brown, plate, 12⁵⁄₁₆ x 9⅝" (30.5 x 24.5 cm)
Collection, The Museum of Modern Art, New York. Given anonymously.
Hofmaier 180 I

Self-Portrait in Bowler Hat. 1921
Drypoint, 12 x 9⅝" (30.5 x 24.5 cm)
Collection, Philadelphia Museum of Art, Purchased: Harrison Fund.
Hofmaier 180 III

powerful head fills the entire sheet, giving the print a sense of monumentality. This work and the masterful *Self-Portrait with Bowler Hat* of 1921 have vital presence, partly due to the heavy burrs of the drypoint, achieved by the laceration of the copper plate. Although the artist is now posed as a gentleman with proper jacket, stiff collar, and necktie and wearing an even stiffer bowler hat, he still appears disturbed as he stares at the viewer in severe frontality. A bright lamp in the first state on the left side of the print is replaced by a sitting cat, and a beer mug and kerosene lamp on the right in the later states of the print. There is also more white, both in the background and in the artist's face, to contrast with the deep black in the hat, eyes, and coat. A *Self-Portrait* of 1922 is one of the rare woodcuts made by the artist, yet he is in full control of the technique. The gouging of the wood corresponds to the grim, almost brutal, appearance of the broad, plebeian head, which is fuller and more rounded than the refined linear drypoint of a year earlier. The large piercing eyes are now narrowed beneath the determined brow, conveying a sense of heroic pride, almost defiance.

MAX BECKMANN

PORTRAIT OF THE ARTIST

Peter Selz

Before the events that led up to World War II, Max Beckmann had been recognized as Germany's foremost painter. But during the Nazis's well-organized purge, 590 of his works were confiscated from museums throughout the nation and he was "featured" in the infamous 1937 "Degenerate Art" exhibition in Munich. Beckmann listened to an inflammatory opening speech on the radio in Berlin, in which Hitler promised imprisonment or sterilization for artists who would persist in their "practice of pre-historic art stutterings," packed his bags, and fled to Amsterdam the next day, never to return to his native land. A year later he went to London to speak at the New Burlington Galleries on the occasion of a memorable exhibition sponsored by Roland Penrose and Herbert Read, "Twentieth-Century German Art." There, in the midst of a highly charged political climate, Beckmann must have surprised his audience by announcing his disinterest in the geopolitical sphere.[1] Instead he emphasized the spiritual realm, the search for the invisible that lies beneath surface reality. He explained the purpose of art as "the quest for our own identity, which transpires on the eternal and obscure path we are bound to travel" and stressed the need to penetrate "the Self…which is the greatest and obscurest secret in the world."[2]

Beckmann's compulsive search for self-revelation in the midst of the horrors perpetrated in his time may seem a shortsighted— and seemingly arrogant—disregard of history. But perhaps his decision to focus on self-exploration is better interpreted as a rejection of the collective dogma and autocratic power that plagued his era. In his self-portraits Beckmann's gaze is at times directed outward, and we see the artist as an observer, voyeur, and chronicler of his life and times. He may look at the viewer with aggressive confrontation; at other times, especially in his drawings, we see a vulnerable, introverted person engaged in painful self-scrutiny.

Beckmann's inward search was no doubt related to his readings of occult and hermetic texts. His early study of Schopenhauer led him to explore the Vedas and Indian philosophy. He perused the Cabala and showed considerable interest in the theosophical teachings of Mme. Blavatsky, whose carefully annotated treatise *The Secret Doctrine* was a prized part of his New York library. Beckmann was also interested in Gnosticism, a religious and philosophical movement that taught revelation through the knowledge and understanding of magical reality and the ineffable experience of the Self. When, in his London lecture, Beckmann spoke of "an intimation of the fourth dimension to which my whole soul aspires," he was not referring to Einstein's much-discussed notion of time, but to the mystical experiences of the soul that preoccupied so many of his contemporaries, including Vasily Kandinsky, Kazimir Malevich, and Piet Mondrian.[3]

Beckmann worked by suggestion and indirection. Like the work of the Symbolist writers and painters, his art operates by evocation. Even during the turbulent period following World War I when the artist felt the need to comment on the horror surrounding him, "to surrender [his] heart and [his] nerves...to the horrible cries of pain of a poor and deluded people,"[4] his paintings were never as outspoken and accusatory as those of such compatriots as George Grosz, Otto Dix, and Rudolf Schlichter. There was always a vital tension between the clear structure of his color and form and the enigmatic nature of his figures and their relationships. Beckmann viewed the physical world as a means of entering the metaphysical realm, and spoke of "realism of the inner visions." His protest against the state of things was not social or political, but religious in nature. Indeed, he once wrote to his friend and publisher Reinhard Piper, "In my paintings I confront God with all he has done wrong....My religion is arrogance before God, defiance of God. Defiance, because he created us so that we cannot love ourselves."[5]

When depicting himself, Beckmann often hid behind multiple roles and disguises. His quest for self-understanding caused him to constantly hold a mirror to his own figure. But rarely does he disclose his soul; instead, he uses the armor of concealment. Beckmann's conception of life as a series of role-playing activities is helpful in understanding this aspect of his work. In a revealing letter to his friend and patron Stephan Lackner, Beckmann expounded his belief that life is a chain of intervals, extending over millions of years, in which each of us personifies a highly individualized but boundlessly versatile actor on the stage of existence.[6] Accordingly, many of his paintings depict stage sets in which figures enact dramatic parts.

Beckmann's use of disguise in his compositions is hardly unique in the history of western art. In early Renaissance paintings, artists such as Masaccio and Botticelli often included themselves among the characters in a sacred composition. Albrecht Dürer, in his idealized Italiante *Self-Portrait* of 1500, depicted himself as no less than the triumphant *Salvator Mundi*, and the young Rembrandt often posed as a nobleman or Oriental prince in sumptuous costumes surrounded by exotic paraphernalia.

In his diaries, Beckmann referred to Dürer and Rembrandt, and even more frequently to van Gogh, who seems to have identified with Christ's martyrdom, while Gauguin (whom Beckmann also respected) portrayed himself with a halo (as well as a snake) in 1899. At the same time James Ensor depicted his own image as the Messiah in his epic canvas *The Entry of Christ into Brussels*. Twenty years later, the young Max

Christ and the Woman Taken in Adultery. 1917
Oil on canvas, 59 x 50⅓" (150 x 128 cm)
Collection, The Saint Louis Art Museum, Bequest of Curt Valentin.
Göpel 197

Beckmann appears as a modern witness—or perhaps already as stage manager—in the large and ambitious painting *Resurrection*. In a very different work of 1917, the figure of the striding and forgiving Saviour in *Christ and the Woman Taken in Adultery* bears a great resemblance to Beckmann himself.

More than any of his contemporaries in the first half of this century, Beckmann saw self-portraiture as a major genre. From his first awkward attempt at age fifteen to his contemplative and wistful final work of 1950, Beckmann produced more than eighty self-portraits in a variety of media, including oil, pen, pencil, crayon, watercolor, drypoint, lithography, woodcut, and bronze. He portrays himself as performer, conjurer, and mountebank, as harlequin and enigmatic prophet. He is king, Homeric hero, and Christ alike. Once, at a masquerade party in St. Louis, wearing a black domino over his eye, he announced facetiously, "I am Jupiter." He poses as the alienated member of his family or seated with a group of friends. He is the man of the world, appearing in tuxedo or tailcoat, the urbane socialite. But he is also the circus barker, the master of ceremonies,

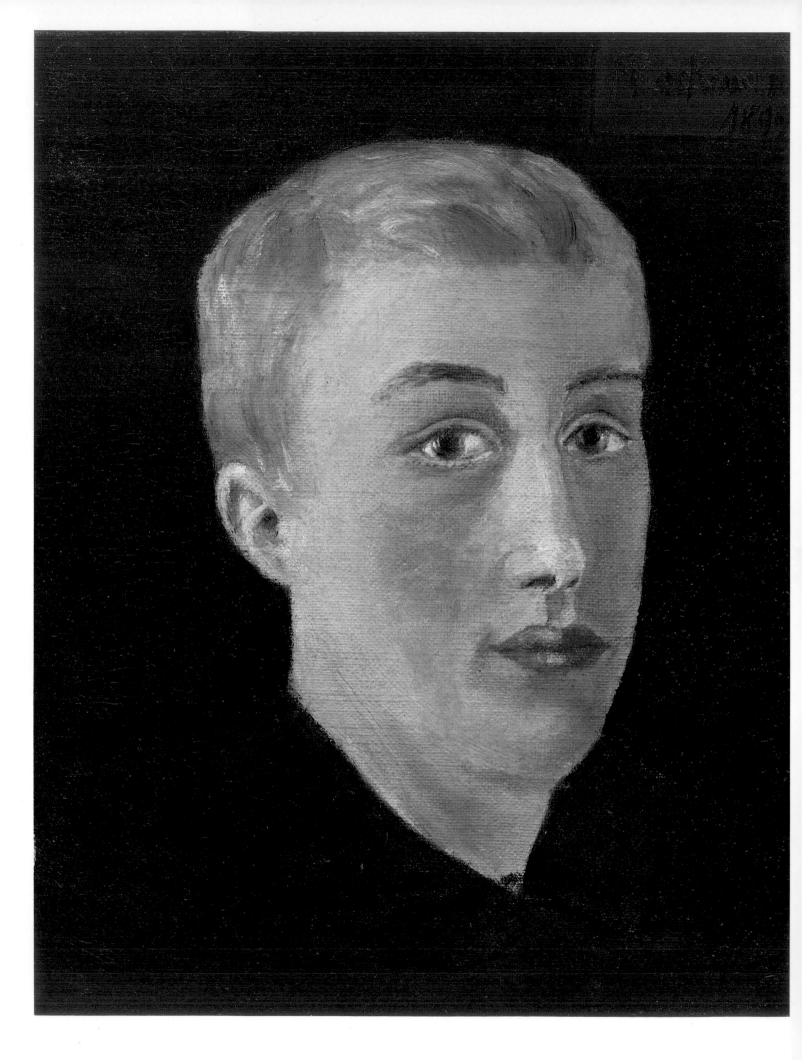

Weimar Academy in 1901, Beckmann made his earliest drypoint—a medium difficult to master but preferred by the artist in later years. He depicts himself screaming—a pose reminiscent of the "character heads" of Franz Xaver Messerschmidt as well as of Edvard Munch's signature canvas.

By 1907 Beckmann presents himself as a well-dressed young man in *Self-Portrait, Florence,* looking at the viewer and the world with a confident, open pose. His large black contour creates a strik-ing contrast to the sunlit Italian landscape seen beyond the window. This is a romantic portrait of the artist as an expectant young man, conscious of early success. Beckmann had just been honored with a purchase award for a painting at the Weimar museum and with a prestigious stipend that sent him to Florence. A few years later he established himself in Berlin and became renowned for his heroic historical compositions *The Destruction of Messina* (1909), *The Battle of the Amazons* (1911), and *The Sinking of the Titanic* (1912). Dubbed the "German Delacroix," Beckmann was by far the youngest artist to be elected to the executive board of the Berlin Secession,

Self-Portrait with Soap Bubbles, 1900
Mixed media on cardboard, 12⅝ x 10" (32 x 25.5 cm)
Private Collection.
Göpel 3

Following pages:
Self-Portrait, Florence, 1907
Oil on canvas, 38⅜ x 35½" (98 x 90 cm)
Collection, Hamburger Kunsthalle, Hamburg.
Göpel 66

Double Portrait Max Beckmann and Minna Beckmann-Tube, 1909
Oil on canvas, 56 x 43" (142 x 109 cm)
Collection, Staatliche Galerie Moritzburg, Halle.
Göpel 109

Self-Portrait, 1899
Oil on canvas, 9¾ x 7½" (25 x 19.5 cm)
Collection, Sprengel Museum, Hannover.
Göpel 1

the hospital attendant, and the persecuted emigrant. Like an actor capable of living a variety of lives by means of dramatic ritual, Beckmann assumes multiple masks to enact and observe the human comedy where truth mixes with illusion. He is the spectator gazing at the world around him, the individual wounded by the journey through a modern inferno.

Beckmann's first self-portrait of 1899, *Self-Portrait,* is a small oil that depicts the adolescent artist with short-cropped blonde hair and lips punctuated by vibrant red paint. His features are still undetermined, his expression that of tentative youth. At about the same time he depicted himself in an armchair, his profile outlined sharply against a lonely North German landscape. He called it *Self-Portrait with Soap Bubbles* and we see him gazing into an unknown distance while the bubbles float toward an autumnal sky. Here the art student, only sixteen years old, locates his work in the European tradition: the theme, signifying the ephemeral nature of existence, has been the subject of the more sophisticated paintings of artists such as Jean Baptiste Chardin and Edouard Manet. While a student at the

In the drypoint *In the Hotel ("The Dollar")* of 1923, Beckmann depicts himself with a mien of disdain at the very thought of a monetary transaction. In this group portrait his dealer, champion, and publisher, J. B. Neumann, seems to be presenting a dollar bill to the artist. A dollar was indeed valuable property at the time, as it was worth one trillion marks in the fall of 1923. This was also the year Neumann moved his gallery to New York with the chief aim of promoting Beckmann's work in America—a task that took much longer than either dealer or artist had anticipated. Neumann looks at the artist with what seems to be an expression of reverence, to which Beckmann responds with a haughty expression. Marta Stern, a woman from the artist's intellectual circle of friends in Frankfurt, witnesses the transaction with apparent concern.

After the mid-twenties, print production tapered off in Beckmann's oeuvre and painting once more took a primary position. In *Self-Portrait with Red Curtain* (1923), he is posed before a heavy red velvet curtain, the traditional backdrop of ruling aristocrats in

Ganze Auflage 21 Abzüge   Rote verndhl

Self-Portrait with Cigarette. 1923
Oil on canvas, 23¾ x 15¾" (60 x 40 cm)
Collection, The Museum of Modern Art, New York. Gift of Dr. and Mrs. F.H. Hirschland.
Göpel 221

Following pages:
Carnival (Pierrette and Clown). 1925
Oil on canvas, 63 x 39⅓" (160 x 100 cm)
Collection, Städtische Kunsthalle, Mannheim.
Göpel 236

Double Portrait Carnival, Max Beckmann and Quappi. 1925
Oil on canvas, 63 x 41½" (160 x 105.5 cm)
Collection, Kunstmuseum der Stadt Düsseldorf, Düsseldorf.
Göpel 240

Baroque portraiture. A mirror with carved molding and a classic motif on the wall behind the artist add to the grandiloquence of the picture. The painter himself, dressed in a tuxedo, wears his bowler hat on the back of his head, and holds a cigar between two outstretched fingers. The red scarf thrown with deliberate casualness around his neck and shoulders matches the curtain. Here he is, the artist as social lion. Later the same year he depicts himself with a more menacing countenance in *Self-Portrait with a Cigarette.* He is now seated against a golden background that is suggestive of medieval paintings. His cubelike head rests uneasily on the massive structure of his body. The stiff collar adds to the sense of rigidity in the work. Hands, which will assume increasing importance in Beckmann's figures, set up a rhythm of their own in front of his body. Cubist formal elements, which enter his syntax for a short time, augment the mask of stern inaccessibility in the painting.

In 1925, shortly before his second marriage to Mathilde von Kaulbach, called "Quappi," Beckmann painted *Carnival*

holding the fish near his face, the eyes of the fish echoing his own. During the same summer, in the Rocky Mountains, Beckmann also drew his *Self-Portrait with Fishing Pole*. He seems to be holding a rope rather than a fishing pole. In the role of a circus performer, he tightly holds the length of rope, which he seems ready to climb at any moment with his powerful arms. His bald head is receding, his mouth is slightly open, his chin sticks out, and his eyes glance defensively at the viewer. In a diary entry from August 27, 1949, his last day in Boulder, he notes the completion of this picture and writes also, "My time has long expired and is prolonged artificially."[31]

Beckmann's last depiction of himself, *Self-Portrait in Blue Jacket*, was painted in his studio on New York's west side during the winter and spring of 1950. The most startling aspect of this late painting is its brilliant color: the unrelenting cobalt blue of the jacket, the bright orange shirt, and the green chair are set against a deep maroon background. The very brightness of the colors contributes to the two-dimensional appearance of the painting: their disparate, almost cruel,

Self-Portrait in Olive and Brown. 1945
Oil on canvas, 23¾ x 19⅝" (60 x 50 cm)
Collection, The Detroit Institute of Arts, Gift of Robert H. Tannahill.
Göpel 705

1909 in his double portrait with his first wife, he expressed a sense of remoteness. Now, thirty-five years later, the two partners in marriage witness each other's solitude. Beckmann holds the inevitable cigarette in his right hand, while the left points toward the netherworld.

On November 29, 1946 Beckmann noted in his diary, "Germany is dying, et moi—Self-Portrait of 1945 is completed."[26] This undoubtedly refers to the small *Self-Portrait in Olive and Brown,* in which he depicts himself at work. Here the artist, dressed like a monk, works in a small, bare room. It is a composition of utmost simplicity. On the left margin of the work is the white canvas on its stretcher in total contrast to its deep black back. Beckmann's massive forehead is lit brightly from above, his lips are set tightly, his eyes are piercing as he works with concentration, observing himself in the mirror, painting his image with the most demanding visual precision.

Day and Dream (1946) was the last suite of prints created by Beckmann. Commissioned by his New York dealer, Curt

Valentin, for the American market, the entire portfolio of fifteen lithographs sold originally for $125.[27] Beckmann made the drawings in Amsterdam and oversaw the printing there. In 1948, now living in St. Louis, he decided to hand-color several of the lithographs that had not been sold. The portfolio, originally called *Time-Motion*, is the closest he ever came to Surrealist imagery. It deals with a variety of motifs, including, in the artist's words, "mythological, biblical, and theatrical subjects and with circus and café of 'all-in-one thing.'"[28] Once again he used a self-portrait for the cover of the suite. Innumerable hatchmarks, going in various directions, give the portrait a dense, sculptural appearance. His hand, holding the ubiquitous cigarette, seems to act as a barrier against the outside world. His eyes, which, as in so many of his self-portraits, are uneven in size, do not look at the spectator but beyond, into an undefined space.

In the summer of 1947 the Beckmanns left Amsterdam for St. Louis, where the artist was invited to teach at Washington University, filling a position vacated by Philip Guston who had traveled

Self-Portrait with Cigarette. 1947
Oil on canvas, 25 x 18" (63.5 x 45.5 cm)
Collection, Museum am Ostwall, Dortmund.
Gopel 752

to Rome on a Guggenheim Fellowship. Guston had admired Beckmann's paintings since he first saw them at Curt Valentin's gallery in 1938, and there is no doubt that the German painter had a significant impact on both the early and the late paintings of Guston. Beckmann had not taught since his dismissal from the Städelsche Kunstinstitut, but with the assistance of Quappi as his translator he was able to communicate with his students. When asked about his attitude toward teaching art, he remarked: "Art cannot be taught, but the way of art can be taught."[29]

During October and November of 1947 he worked in St. Louis on his *Self-Portrait with Cigarette*. A brilliantly painted green scarf is draped with deliberate casualness around his neck. The everpresent cigarette emits a wonderful curl of smoke near his left eye. The eyes look with defiance at the viewer. There is an attitude of remote wariness about his self-image, in spite of the enthusiastic welcome he had received in the art community of St. Louis: A major retrospective was in preparation at the St. Louis Art Museum and his work was being exhibited

The Liberated. 1937
Oil on canvas, 23½ x 15¾" (60 x 40 cm)
Private Collection.
Göpel 476

he seems to practically slip off the stairs—and his dark eyes appear again to look pensively into empty space.

Soon after reaching exile in Holland, Beckmann revised an earlier canvas of 1933 in which he presents himself as a golden king. The original figure, with its stern expression of pride, may have been related to the artist's youthful admiration of the Nietzschean concept of artist as superman, but the final version, *The King* (1937), with its inward withdrawal, may indicate Beckmann's increasing interest in the Gnostic belief in the royal origin of the soul. The addition of the wheel to the composition may also be a reference to the Buddha, who put the wheel of sacred teaching into motion.[16] Beckmann filled every inch of space, "that frightening and unthinkable inversion of the Force of the Universe,"[17] with people and objects. The vulnerable king himself is guarded by a figure resembling Quappi, as well as by a mighty protective sword. A short time later the artist visualized himself as a persecuted refugee in *The Liberated* (1937). In this highly revealing canvas Beckmann has unchained

Couple by the Window. 1937
Oil on canvas, 23½ x 15¾" (59.5 x 40 cm)
Collection, Stephan and Margaret Lackner.
Göpel 473

himself from imaginary manacles that cuffed his hands and bound his neck to prison bars. The pained and tragic expression on his face, the picture's dark and somber coloration, and the black fateful area behind the window are not signifiers of liberation and freedom, but of death. It could only have been Beckmann's deep sense of irony that caused him to call this small canvas *The Liberated*.

In 1937 Beckmann also furnished seven lithographs to illustrate the Paris edition of the play *Der Mensch ist kein Haustier* by his friend Stephan Lackner. Lackner had begun acquiring paintings when he first managed to see a censored exhibition by the artist in 1933 and became an important patron of the painter during their years in exile. The play deals with revolution, the class struggle and the foundation of a technocratic state. The small vertical painting, *Couple by the Window* (1937), is closely related to one of the lithographs. In both versions, the male figure appears to be a self-portrait of the artist. Here he has identified himself with the brutal murderer, Peter Giel, a man from the underworld, with

Self-Portrait with Horn. 1938
Oil on canvas, 43¼ x 39¾" (110 x 101 cm)
Private Collection.
Göpel 489

whom the beautiful princess Louise had fallen in love. In the painting, the dark dominant male figure in the background creates a striking contrast to the light-skinned, angular image of the young woman fixing her hair.

The sense of despair revealed in *Self-Portrait with Crystal Ball* and in *The Liberated* is deepened in the 1938 *Self-Portrait with Horn.* He depicts himself again in prison garb, and holds an instrument in his hands. Now in exile, however, Beckmann's American saxophone becomes a German trumpet, which he holds close to his ear listening to what secret message it may have to reveal as he gazes into darkness with melancholy eyes, set again into dark cavities. His head is surrounded by an empty golden frame, which may denote a painting or a mirror. Although the artist's torso is strong and powerful, the painting relays a sense of dark mystery and veiled desperation.

In May 1940 the German army invaded Holland, making the émigré's life hazardous. In the fall he painted *Acrobat on Trapeze,* a canvas at once connoting this peril and a surprisingly optimistic view of

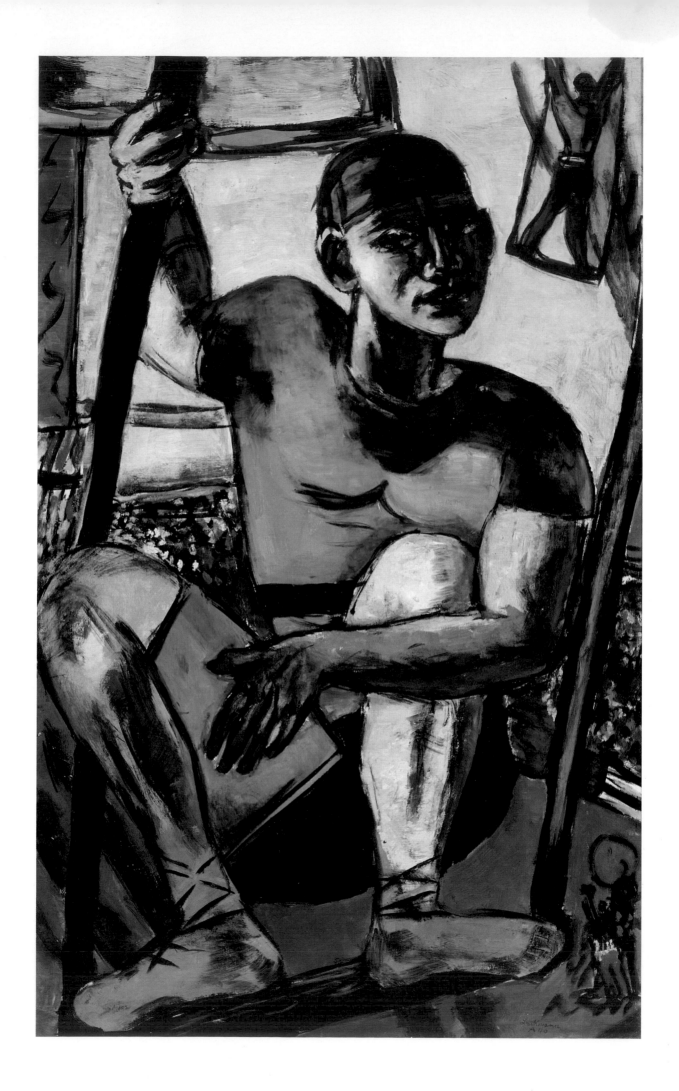

Acrobat on Trapeze. 1940
Oil on canvas, 57½ x 35½" (146 x 90 cm)
Collection, The Saint Louis Art Museum, Bequest of Morton D. May.
Göpel 547

his difficult situation. Although Beckmann's widow has stated this painting was not, in fact, a self-portrait,[18] the features on the equilibrist's face appear to be self-referential. Although high in the air, the acrobat's feet are planted firmly on the footboard, implying a sense of safety in the midst of potential danger. Eight years later at Stephens College, Beckmann concluded his renowned lecture "Letters to a Woman Painter" saying, "We are all tightrope walkers. With them it is the same as with artists, and with all mankind. As the Chinese philosopher Laotse says, we have 'the desire to achieve balance and to keep it.'"[19]

In *Self-Portrait with Green Curtain* of the same year, however, the artist faces his mirror and his viewers with an expression of bitter desolation. He has just made an abrupt turn of the head to confront the spectator, while his torso is still seen from the back. Any action is thwarted by the lack of arms, leaving the figure in a state of impotence. Most of the artist's masklike face is hidden in dark shadow, but the left part is revealed in a harsh, blinding light. His eyes seem unable to focus. The curtain behind the figure with its many x-figurations increases the painting's deep sense of mystery. This seems to have been a period of despondence for the artist, who noted in his diary, "I apparently must live, am sentenced to living by some unknown power that finds this inevitable."[20]

Beckmann was not, however, alone in exile. His wife provided some comfort from the alienation that increasingly enveloped his life. In the 1941 *Double Portrait of Max Beckmann and Quappi,* the couple is elegantly attired as world travelers. This narrow, stele-like painting recalls the *Double Portrait Carnival* of sixteen years earlier. Although Beckmann's large figure seems to crowd his wife out of the picture, she is still guiding him through an alien world.

It was in his triptychs, with all their complexities, that Beckmann's genius in structuring intricate compositions and his command of sonorous colors that recall medieval stained glass became most evident. Here he addresses human cruelty, passion, anguish and liberation, and the ceaseless search for the Self. The great, continuing potency of these

works is partly due to the ambivalence of the allusions and the inexhaustible richness of their multiple references.

Beckmann began working on *The Actors* in May 1941 and completed the triptych in July 1942. In the middle of the central panel we see the king in the play thrusting a sword into his own heart. There is a general agreement that this theater king is indeed an enigmatic self-portrait of the artist as a younger man enacting his own suicide. But what is the reason for this act of desperation? Friedhelm Fischer suggests that it is a portentous metaphor of the desperate role played by the dedicated artist, who takes his task deadly serious.[21] In Gnosticism the body is the earthly shell for the kingly self. And in this painting the king commits suicide as the final shattering sign of contempt, the ultimate protest against the forces of fate. Gert Schiff, in his perspicacious discussion of this triptych, relates the central theme to one of Beckmann's favorite novels, Jean Paul's *The Titan*. Schiff argues that Beckmann identified with the book's demonic antagonist Roquairol, and "used him as a parable of the artist, who

The Actors. 1941-1942
Oil on canvas, center: 78¾ x 59" (200 x 150 cm)
Wings: 78¾ x 33½" (200 x 85 cm)
Collection, Harvard University Art Museums, Gift of Lois Orswell.
Göpel 604

also 'contrives' his strongest passions, and exhibits his deepest wounds in his work, and for the same reason is deprived of a life of his own."[22]

Les Artistes with Vegetables (1943) depicts an imaginary gathering of the artist with three friends during their lonely years in exile in Amsterdam. Their encounter is imagined, as Beckmann would meet with them only individually. They are, in fact, not engaged in casual table conversation, but each man seems to be absorbed in his own thought and fate. There is a feeling of unspoken ritual in this painting. Each of the men except Beckmann himself holds an edible object. In the lower left Friedrich Vordemberge-Gildewart, the constructivist painter and Beckmann's closest confidante during this period, holds a parsnip—the only vegetable in the painting, despite its title. Next to him, wearing a fur hat and scarf, is the painter Herbert Fiedler[23] holding a fish. Fiedler, whom Beckmann had known during his Berlin days, was a frequent companion of the artist in Amsterdam. On Beckmann's right we see the poet Wolfgang Frommel, who holds a loaf of bread in an almost sacrificial gesture. Frommel, a disciple of

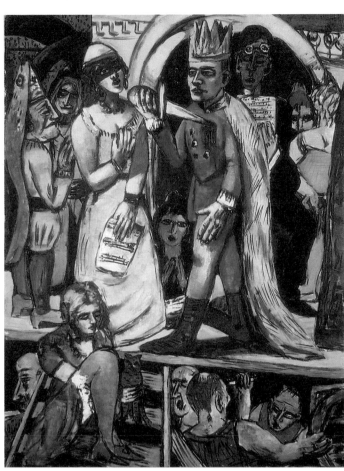

Les Artistes with Vegetables (Four Men Around a Table). 1943
Oil on canvas, 59 x 45½" (150 x 115.5 cm)
Collection, Washington University Gallery of Art, St. Louis,
University purchase, Kende Sale Fund, 1946.
Göpel 626

the Symbolist poet Stefan George, was also a student of alchemical texts and a person whose company was important to Beckmann during this period. A large mirror or painting is on the wall behind the poet's head. These are men with whom Beckmann was often engaged in serious discussion about everything from the political situation during the war to the meaning of life and theories of the cosmos. Beckmann himself is clutching a mirror that reflects a distorted mask, or possibly the face of a foolish painted clown. The mirror may be a reference to the *Seelenspiegel,* or "mirror of the soul," that appears in the romantic literature of E. T. A. Hoffmann and Jean Paul, German writers whose work Beckmann read with frequency. In the center of the white table and directly above the mirror, creating a central vertical axis, is a flickering candle, a sign of light and a symbol of truth, but also of temporal existence. These men seem to be meeting secretly at night. They are crowded together and a sense of unease is enhanced by the tilt of both floor and table. It seems unlikely, knowing Beckmann and his three emigrant friends, that they are engaged in an underground resistance

Self-Portrait in Black. 1944
Oil on canvas, 37½ x 23½" (95 x 60 cm)
Collection, Bayerische Staatsgemäldesammlungen, Munich.
Göpel 655

conspiracy. It seems, rather, that Beckmann has assembled these men in this ritualistic setting at the round table as a foregathering of an intellectual elite of artists. "Art," he wrote earlier, "is the mirror of God, embodied by man."[24]

The mask he assumes in *Self-Portrait in Black* of 1944 is that of Mephistophelian power and darkness. During a period of ten months prior to this work, Beckmann executed a series of 143 draw-ings for Goethe's *Faust II* for a Frankfurt typefounder—a commission that helped support the artist during this difficult time in exile. In this painting that relates to the *Faust* drawings, Beckmann throws himself aggressively against the viewer. He has placed his large left arm over the chair back while he simultaneously pulls his forearm and hand against the curtain. The figure seems to describe a virtual circle. The chair and the velvet cur-tain suggest that he is seated in the loge of a theater. His masklike head, mostly in shadow, presents a stony countenance with tightly closed lips and piercing eyes challenging the viewer. There is no access to this man, who seems totally armored against human contact. Once more, he is

Double Portrait Max and Quappi Beckmann. 1944
Pen and ink, 15½ x 9¼" (39.5 x 23.5 cm)
Collection, Perry T. Rathbone.

dressed in dark formal wear, but this painting lacks the self-assurance of the 1927 self-portrait or the wistfulness of the 1937 painting. Instead, he sees himself as a sinister individual, a modern Mephisto who contends that life is worthless and must be destroyed; at this time Beckmann referred to himself as "the spirit that eternally denies." On December 27, 1943, the artist's journal entry reads: "In the morning completed Self-Portrait with arm over the back of chair...Deprimé." And a few days later, on New Year's Eve, "Dark is life...is Death."[25]

The tragedy of human existence is also evident in a drawing of himself and his wife—*Double Portrait Max and Quappi Beckmann* (1944). He stands in the frontal plane, facing the viewer, wearing a Jacobin cap. To his left, at a right angle, is Quappi in severe profile, carrying their dog Butchy in her right arm. A few lines, indicating a boxlike room, frame their bodies. Husband and wife are in close proximity but do not look at each other. Their faces are dark. They are silent, although as his style has changed, there is consistency of meaning in Beckmann's work. As early as

Self-Portrait in Sailor Hat. 1926
Oil on canvas, 39⅕ x 28" (100 x 71 cm)
Collection, ADF International Co./F. Elghanayan, New York.
Göpel 262

(Pierrette and Clown). The artist has masked himself by wrapping his face in a white cowl[11] and sits with his legs stretched high in the air—a most unusual position. His new wife stands nearby dressed as Pierrette, paying no attention to the buffoon beside her. Although the artist often spoke of his happiness in the new marriage, this picture, with its attitude of weary distance rendered in icy colors, gives us little sense of joy. As in the closely related *Double Portrait Carnival* painted later that year, mask and pose are used as devices to reveal the sense of doubt and loneliness that plagued the artist even during good times. In *Carnival* we see the couple on stage in a carnival tent. The artist, his face painted white, appears as Watteau's *Gilles*, while his new wife, riding an elaborately carved hobbyhorse, seems to be guiding the pair to an unknown destination. As well as gauging Beckmann's psychological state at the time, this work shows the influence of the school of Magic Realism, an international movement in the 1920s that explored the alogical, metaphysical world by transposing dreamlike objects into paintings that were astonishing in their realistic rendering.

Beckmann appears in an entirely different pose in his 1927 canvas *Self-Portrait in Tuxedo*, undoubtedly the most magisterial portrait of his oeuvre. Instead of the angst-ridden jester of the 1925 paintings, we now see before us a formidable figure in full career bloom. He was married to a beautiful young woman with important social connections. He had an impressive number of solo exhibitions with the renowned Flechtheim Gallery in Düsseldorf and received an annual stipend from the New York–based J. B. Neumann. He was appointed to a professorship at the Städelsche Kunstinstitut in Frankfurt and in the same year was represented at the prestigious Venice Biennale. Germany had achieved a new sense of economic and socio-political stability, and Beckmann took this opportunity to write an erudite text on "The Artist in the State." "As the conscious shaper of the transcendental idea," and "of vital significance to the state,"[12] he asserted an identification of man with God, stipulating with seeming irony, "the new priests of this new cultural center must be dressed in dark suits or on state occasions appear in tuxedo, unless we succeed

Self-Portrait with Saxophone. 1930
Oil on canvas, 55 x 27⅓" (140 x 69.5 cm)
Collection, Bremen Kunsthalle, Bremen.
Göpel 320

in developing an even more precise and elegant piece of manly attire. Workers, moreover, should likewise appear in tuxedo or tails. Which is to say: we seek a new kind of aristocratic Bolshevism. A social equalization, the fundamental principle of which, however, is not the satisfaction of pure materialism, but rather the conscious and organized drive to become God ourselves." In this elegant canvas, Beckmann confronts the viewer hand on hip in a stance, according to Stephan Lackner, "reminiscent of the classical contrapposto of heroic statues."[13] But behind this image of the modern aristocratic visionary and his immaculate exterior, the sharper play of light and shadow, the contrast of large planes of black and areas of blinding white, suggest an underlying tension and inquietude.

In successive self-portraits during the remainder of his successful Frankfurt years, Beckmann presents himself in a variety of guises. We see him in 1930, in *Self-Portrait with Saxophone*, standing on a narrow stage, dressed in athletic garb and bathrobe, holding a saxophone in his large hands. The saxophone is an allusion to the jazz music

Beckmann had grown to appreciate for its novelty and innovation. Writing to his publisher Reinhard Piper in 1923, Beckmann confessed, "I love jazz, especially because of cowbells and automobile horns. That is sensible music. What one could do with it!"[14] The saxophone, which also appears in several still lifes of this period, has been interpreted by some as a symbol of the life force[15] that sustained Beckmann through hard times. Certainly music in general was of great importance to the artist; he wrote early in his career about his admiration for Bach and Mozart, and both his wives were accomplished musicians.

The bright, dissonant colors that help create the mood of vitality in *Self-Portrait with Saxophone* shift to an icier palette in *Self-Portrait in Hotel* of 1932. There Beckmann stands, his head in dark shadow, a cold, forlorn individual in coat, hat, and scarf, hands jammed in pockets. He is pressed into an exceedingly narrow space with mirrors in wall and ceiling that reflect his image at the hotel's entrance. A recurring theme in modern German literature and art, the hotel is a place for wealthy travelers

Self-Portrait in Hotel. 1932
Oil on canvas, 46½ x 19¾" (118.5 x 50.5 cm)
Private Collection.
Göpel 359

and homeless transients alike. It is a meeting place for businessmen as well as for intellectuals. It is at once the site of open communication and of meaningless anomie. Beckmann himself found the hotel to be a place of continuous fascination, a locus where he could observe and be observed. During his Frankfurt years he would often go to the Hotel Monopol-Metropole near the Central Railroad Station, and toward the end of his life in New York he frequented the Plaza.

Fast approaching the age of fifty, Beckmann's thoughts turned to life's transience, as can be seen in a Vanitas picture entitled *Self-Portrait in Large Mirror with Candle*. Ever since the 16th century, the burning candle has been used as an allegory of mortality, and in this 1933 canvas a green table in the foreground bears the artist's glasses, two bottles, a plant with large leaves and small white blossoms, a burning red candle, and a book opened to reveal an illustration of the planet Saturn. The word "Saturn" had also made its appearance in the *Large Still-Life with Telescope* of 1927, and seems to have been of special significance to the painter. The

Self-Portrait with Black Cap. 1934
Oil on canvas, 39⅓ x 27½" (100 x 70 cm)
Collection, Museum Ludwig, Cologne.
Göpel 391

capricious planet, with its singular relationship to artists and magicians, held a unique attraction to the hermetic painter, who himself was born under the sign of Saturn. In the large mirror, denoting vanity, we see the black shadow of Beckmann's powerful profile against a red curtain with the swordlike leaf of the plant cutting across his forehead.

The rise in power of National Socialism in Germany disrupted Beckmann's art production and left a disturbing mark on what work he did execute. Less a magician now than a humble artist, Beckmann wears the traditional garb of the artist in *Self-Portrait with Black Cap.* Painted after the artist was dismissed from his professorship by the Nazis, Beckmann stands defiantly with arms crossed in front of his chest in self-protection. With an expression of dejection Beckmann is obviously pondering the future in the *Self-Portrait with Crystal Ball* of 1936—the year in which the Nazis closed the room dedicated to his work in the Berlin Nationalgalerie, and the atrocities of Hitler reached new extremes. The artist holds a large crystal ball in his hand. Dominated by

greenish-blue colors, *Self-Portrait with Crystal Ball* is based on the geometry of the sphere: the roundness of the ball is echoed in the half circles of shoulder and lips and again in the artist's forehead, as well as in the dark, almost sinister, cavities of his eyes. Beckmann's eyes do not look into the crystal ball, nor are they directed at the viewer. Their gaze goes beyond, into an unknown and threatening future. Although the artist holds the means of divination in his very hands, he is helpless and seems to recede into the deep black space behind him.

Shortly before leaving Germany Beckmann depicted himself once more as a member of high society in *Self-Portrait in Tails*, which is in sharp distinction to the 1927 *Self-Portrait in Tuxedo*. The 1937 canvas, with its extended vertical shape and bright color contrasts, is a disquieting picture. The self-assurance of ten years earlier has given way to an almost palpable unease. The sovereign posture of the hands has been replaced by a striking downward gesture. And these hands are now huge, pawlike hanging forms. The stance of the artist is very unsteady —

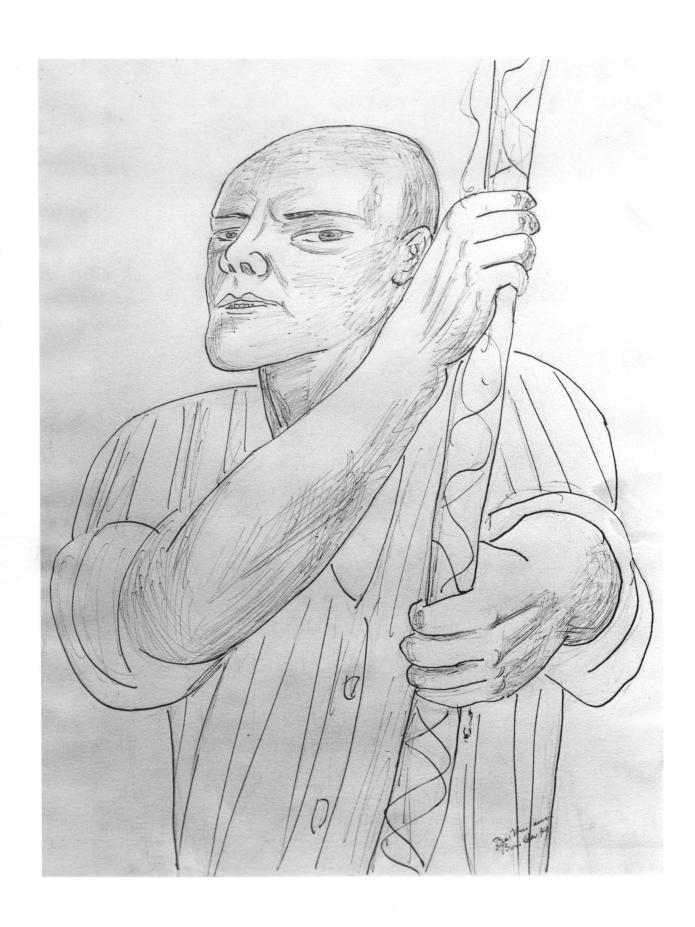

Self-Portrait with Fishing Pole. 1949
Pen, ink and pencil on white paper, 23¾ x 18" (60 x 45.5 cm)
The University of Michigan Museum of Art, Acc. No. 1950/1.159.

Following page:
Self-Portrait in Blue Jacket. 1950
Oil on canvas, 55 x 36" (139.5 x 91.5 cm)
Collection, The Saint Louis Art Museum, Bequest of Morton D. May.
Göpel 816

quality give an insolent air to this wistful, contemplative figure. He looks drawn and tired, but still defiant. He no longer assumes roles or disguises. There is no artifice in this picture, and there are no props. He stands alone, leaning against the chair back, drawing on a cigarette as if for nourishment. The large, penetrating eyes of Beckmann, always the observer, are alert. On the left, extending the whole height of the painting, looms the frightening black emptiness of space. But the large surface directly behind the painter is yet another newly stretched canvas ready for his work. Beckmann had to go on painting no matter how apparently meaningless his existence. For him painting was more than an aesthetic enterprise. It was a moral act, a means to come to terms with what he termed the "mystery of being," with ultimate reality. Toward the end of his life Beckmann wrote in a letter to a friend: "The moral principle is not to be avoided. Ever since ancient Indian wisdom, since the Gnostics and the Essenes, and on to Kant and Schopenhauer, it has always been the same and cannot be denied."[32]

NOTES

1 Max Beckmann, "On my Painting," lecture at the New Burlington Galleries, London, 1938. In *Max Beckmann* (exh. cat.), London, 1974, pp. 11-21. This is the text of a lecture Beckmann delivered at the New Burlington Galleries in London in 1938. It was originally written in German and translated into English soon thereafter in a cursory translation first published in *Centaur* (vol. I, No. 6, pp. 287-292) in Amsterdam in 1946. This text was then translated back into German and appeared in the first post-World War II monograph on the artist: Benno Reifenberg and Wilhelm Hausentein, *Max Beckmann* (Munich, R. Piper Verlag), 1949, pp. 47-54. The original German version was published in Peter Beckmann and Peter Selz, *Max Beckmann: Sichtbares und Unsichtbares* (Stuttgart, Belser Verlag, 1965) pp. 20-33. This was translated by P. S. Falla for the Marlborough Gallery catalogue of 1974 and the quotations in this essay are from that translation.

2 *Ibid*, p. 19.

3 Friedhelm Wilhelm Fischer, *Max Beckmann: Symbol und Weltbild*, Munich, 1972; and Fischer, *Max Beckmann*, London, 1973.

4 Beckmann in Kasimir Edschmidt, ed., "Schöpferische Konfession." In *Tribüne der Kunst und Zeit*, vol. 13 (1920), pp. 62-67; transl. in Victor H. Meisel, ed., *Voices of German Expressionism*, Englewood Cliffs, N.J., 1970, p. 108.

5 Beckmann in Reinhard Piper, *Erinnerungen an Max Beckmann*, Munich, 1950, p. 33.

6 Beckmann in Stephan Lackner, *Ich erinnere mich gut an Max Beckmann*, Mainz, 1967, p. 88.

7 *Ibid*, p. 96.

8 Beckmann, *Briefe im Kriege*, Berlin, 1916, letter of May 24, 1915.

9 *Ibid*, letter of October 30, 1914.

10 James D. Burke, "Max Beckmann: An Introduction to his Self-Portraits." In Carla Schulz-Hoffmann, ed., *Max Beckmann*, St. Louis, 1984, p. 58.

11 The art historian Benno Reifenberg remembered seeing Beckmann dressed in a similar costume at a masked ball in Frankfurt. Reifenberg in Erhard and Barbara Göpel, *Max Beckmann: Katalog der Gemälde*, vol. I, Bern, 1976, p. 174.

12 Beckmann, "The Artist and the State." In Hans Belting, *Max Beckmann*, New York, 1989, p. 113.

13 Stephan Lackner, *Max Beckmann*, New York, 1977, p. 98.

14 Beckmann in a letter to Reinhard Piper, March 12. In *Die Realität der Träume in den Bildern, Aufzätzen und Vorträgen 1903-1950*, Leipzig, 1987, p. 102. It is probable that Beckmann referred less to original New Orleans jazz than to modern composers such as Edgard Varèse and Darius Milhaud, who incorporated such city noises into their work.

15 Fischer, *Max Beckmann: Symbol und Weltbild*, Munich, 1972, p. 81.

16 *Ibid*, p. 133.

17 Beckmann, "Letters to a Woman Painter." In Peter Selz, *Max Beckmann*, New York, 1964, p. 132.

18 Mathilde Q. Beckmann in an interview with the author, New York, December 1963.

19 Beckmann, "Letter to a Woman Painter," *op. cit.*, p. 134.

20 Beckmann, *Tagebücher 1940-1950*, Munich, 1979, p. 26.

21 Fischer, *Max Beckmann: Symbol und Weltbild*, Munich, 1972, pp. 162-165.

22 Gert Schiff, "The Nine Triptychs of Max Beckmann." In *Max Beckmann: The Triptychs* (exh. cat.), London, 1980, p. 18.

23 Göpel has identified this individual as Herbert Fiedler rather than as the theater manager Ludwig Berger, as named by Gotthard Jedlicka in "Max Beckmann in seinen Selbstbildnissen." In *Blick auf Beckmann*, p. 129.

24 Beckmann in "The Artist in the State." In Belting, *op. cit.*, p. 113.

25 Beckmann, *Tagebücher 1940-1950*, p. 77.

26 *Ibid*, p. 144.

27 Karen F. Beall, "Max Beckmann Day and Dreams." In *The Quarterly Journal of Library of Congress*, January 1970, p. 8.

28 Beckmann in a letter to Curt Valentin, March 1, 1946. In the Museum of Modern Art Archives.

29 Beckmann in Dorothy Seckler, "Can Painting Be Taught?" *Art News*, L:1 (1951), p. 231.

30 Beckmann, *Tagebücher 1940-1950*, p. 231.

31 Beckmann, *Tagebücher 1940-1950*, p. 346.

32 Beckmann in a letter to Elizabeth Kerschbaumer. In Fritz Erpel, *Max Beckmann*, East Berlin, 1985, p. 93.

Self-Portrait. 1918
Drypoint, 10⅞ x 9⅞" (27.5 x 25 cm)
Private Collection.

NATHAN OLIVEIRA

Afterword

I met Max Beckmann in a summer session at Mills College in Oakland in 1950, the year he died. I was a student, and in so many ways that simple encounter set things straight for me.

I was studying at the California College of Arts and Crafts, a good little art school. It wasn't as important as the Art Institute in San Francisco where all the modern painters taught—Clyfford Still, Mark Rothko—painters who were revolutionizing the art world. I was at this art school that still trained people how to paint the figure and other fairly traditional concerns. I had reached a point where this wasn't enough for me, and I didn't know how to get to the next level. How was I going to connect with the contemporary world? As a formalist painter, I didn't have any credibility with Still and Rothko.

Things first started happening for me around 1949, when three major retrospective exhibitions opened at the M.H. de Young Museum in San Francisco—Oskar Kokoschka, Edvard Munch, and Max Beckmann. I was overwhelmed by all three because they were dealing with a modern language of paint and gesture, far more contemporary than I had ever seen. It was much more agreeable to me than Picasso or Matisse. I loved Picasso and Matisse, but I found a greater sympathy to the European Expressionists. So when I found out that Beckmann was going to be teaching at Mills College I decided to go there.

I was ready, because I somehow thought that if I met this man, in whose work I found a certain sympathy, I could find out more about myself. I wasn't disappointed. Beckmann was very European, very German. He looked imposing, and reminded me of busts of Beethoven; a very serious man. He and his wife Quappi would walk around the campus, and he would carry a little dog. I always associated Max Beckmann with this dog. Because he spoke very little English, his wife—who was known as his translator—would say to the artists, "We'd like to see you use more black," or, "We'd like to see you do this or that." Beckmann himself would make an effort to say a few things, although he was not all that enthused about engaging the students. He seemed like a very fundamental man, whose only interest was in painting—that's all he wanted to do. Still, I think from our encounters he communicated, indirectly, what artistic values were about.

His classes were made up of some of those abstract expressionist students from the Art Institute, for whom he had little sympathy. They were full of themselves and modern painting, and had come to work with Beckmann, maintaining this posture. There were also a few little old women who were painting backyard impressionism, and who shouldn't have been there at all. Then there were people like myself, figurative painters who had a sense of what the figure was about but didn't know how to make it into anything else. He would walk around, and kind of smile at the ladies and say, "Not bad, not bad," or nothing at all. And then he would come to the abstract expressionists and say, "Amusing, amusing, very amusing," and walk off. Then he would come around to me, or a couple of the others painting figuratively, and still he had very little to contribute. Things were kind of forced, but he would look and try to be serious about the work. My paintings fluctuated from inventive, expressive figures to straight realism. He got more enthused about the reality of things. Once I was painting the corner of the studio and he thought that was good. That dealt with a certain credibility, and from this I could progress into something that would be more personalized, but this was the way to get to it. I found this to be a lesson of importance.

I found the issue of figuration to be important as well; and from this encounter with Beckmann, I found he had little sympathy for abstract painting. He was absolutely out of the style of his day, yet this supported a kind of personal energy that I shared too. In a sense he was saying, 'Deal with reality and you'll find something for yourself.'

Once he was walking around the classroom studio, and there was a woman painting a quaint house with picket fence and flowers, a small canvasboard picture. I think he'd just reached a point where he couldn't handle it. She was nagging him about something and he looked at her, then went into this dirty turpentine with a big brush. She thought, Well, he's going to clean his brush and go in there and do something—really transform this into a masterpiece. He splashed out the turpentine and made a big puddle of black on this palette, spilling over into all the other colors. Suddenly she got this look of horror on her face, where she didn't quite know what he was going to do. He just went across the painting, saying, "More black," and destroyed it. He had very little patience. In some ways it was sort of sad, but on the other hand it made issues very clear. He wasn't there to fool around with amateurs, holding hands and patting them on the back.

Another time we were downstairs in the museum looking at his show, and I wanted to know what it took to paint. I went up to him and I said, "What does it mean to paint, what does it take to paint, and what do I have to do?" He said, "Sweat, much sweat." Hard work, you know, that was it. But it was enough, because at that time I was already discovering how to press your own personal issues. It wasn't simply a matter of riding on inspiration, or just letting anything go.

Beckmann symbolized the old world. Tradition, yes, but on the other hand renewing tradition—in the sense that the past wasn't being thrown away. It was as if he were saying, 'This is it, this tradition, but I'm now dealing with my own reality.' Beckmann starts out with a reality which is very fundamental. Over a period of years, and through many periods of transition, you see his work become more and more personalized, and the image becomes very particular. I picked that up and that's pretty much what I based my own work on.

As I said, Beckmann pretty much set things straight for me. It was teaching through example as much as anything, seeing the sincerity there. And I think if anybody wanted to learn from him, that's what he was going to tell you. He didn't articulate visual relationships, or criticism. It was simply his example as an artist. He was the first major figure that I had encountered, and it made everything very clear.

Boy, weren't his paintings beautiful! Those incredible fish, and acrobats and trapeze artists; and these self-portraits which were so quiet and so strong. There was a power that was emanating from his painting that was far more potent than what I was recognizing in most things I was seeing, and I wanted this. That made sense to me, that was the influence.

I was concerned with drama, and this was another thing I got from Beckmann. He could manipulate reality; he wasn't satisfied with just looking and observing. His work had a dramatic power. I couldn't figure out the images, or didn't quite understand intellectually what it all meant, except that these were all inventions that grew out of the act of painting. This gave me a great deal of support for my own immature feelings about the validity of abstract painting. No matter what I painted, if it was totally abstract, it simply would not hold water. But as soon as the work became figurative, or something recognizable, then it made more sense. Beckmann supported that kind of groundwork, and supported the seriousness of this pursuit and this demeanor. He was pivotal to me because he assured me that the solutions were within myself, that I didn't have to go following after abstract worlds.

As Schoenberg said, "Everything is tradition, tradition is everything" — because it's continually renewable, in how you see it, learn from it, and then pass it on. It isn't a matter of simply repeating it, but somehow taking the responsibility of tradition and taking it a step further. In this sense, Beckmann was a classical artist.

BIBLIOGRAPHY

Monographs

Beckmann, Mathilde Q. *Mein Leben mit Max Beckmann.*
Translated from the English by Doris Schmidt.
Munich, 1963.

Beckmann, Peter. *Max Beckmann.* Nürnberg, 1955.
_____. *Max Beckmann, Leben und Werk,* Stuttgart, 1982.
_____. (ed.) *Sichtbares und Unsichtbares.* Intro. by Peter
Selz, Stuttgart, 1965.

Blick auf Beckmann: Dokumente und Vorträge (ed. by Hans
Martin Frhr. von Erffa and Erhard Göpel.) Munich,
1962.

Belting, Hans. *Max Beckmann.* Preface by Peter Selz.
New York, 1989.

Buchheim, Lothar-Günter. *Max Beckmann.* Feldafing,
1959.

Busch, Günter. *Max Beckmann Eine Einführung,* Munich,
1960.

Eberle, Matthias. *Max Beckmann. Die Nacht.* Frankfurt
(Main), 1984.

Erpel, Fritz. *Max Beckmann.* Berlin (DDR), 1981.

Fischer, Friedhelm Wilhelm. *Max Beckmann: Symbol und
Weltbild.* Munich, 1972.
_____. *Max Beckmann.* Translated by P.S. Falla. New
York, 1973.

Gallwitz, Klaus. *Max Beckmann Die Druckgraphik.*
Karlsruhe, 1962.
_____. *Max Beckmann.* Stuttgart, 1990.
_____. *Max Beckmann in Frankfurt.* Frankfurt (Main),
1984.

Glaser, Kurt; Meier-Graefe, Julius; Fraenger, Wilhelm
and Hausenstein, Wilhelm. *Max Beckmann.* Munich,
1924.

Göpel, Erhard. *Max Beckmann der Maler.* Munich, 1954.
_____. *Max Beckmann der Zeichner.* Munich 1954.
_____. *Max Beckmann in seinen späten Jahren.* Munich,
1955.
_____. and Barbara Göpel. *Max Beckmann: Katalog der
Gemälde* (2 vols) Bern, 1976.

Güse, Ernst-Gerhard. *Das Frühwerk Max Beckmanns.*
Frankfurt (Main), 1977.

Hofmaier, James. *Max Beckmann, Catalogue Raisonné of
his Prints* (2 vols) Bern, 1990.

Kaiser, Hans. *Max Beckmann*. Berlin, 1913.

Kaiser, Stephan. *Max Beckmann*. Stuttgart, 1962.

Kessler, Charles S. *Max Beckmann's Triptychs*. Cambridge, MA, 1970.

Lackner, Stephan. *Ich erinnere mich gut an Max Beckmann*. Mainz, 1967.
_____. *Max Beckmann 1884-1950*. Berlin, 1962.
_____. *Max Beckmann*. New York, 1977.
_____. *Max Beckmann: Memories of a Friendship*. Coral Gables, 1969.
_____. *Max Beckmann Triptychen*. Berlin, 1965.

Lenz, Christian. *Max Beckmann: Ewig wechselndes Welttheater*. Esslingern, 1984.

Piper, Reinhard. *Nachmittag, Erinnerungen eines Verlegers*. Munich, 1950.

Reifenberg, Benno and Hausentein, Wilhalm. *Max Beckmann*. Munich, 1949.

Roh, Franz. *Max Beckmann als Maler*. Munich, 1946.

Schöne, Wolfgang. *Max Beckmann*. Berlin, 1947.

Schulz-Hoffman, Carla and Weiss, Judith C. (eds.) *Max Beckmann Retrospektive*. Munich/St. Louis, 1984.
_____. *Max Beckmann*. Munich, 1992.

Selz, Peter. *Max Beckmann*. New York, 1964.

Simon, Heinrich. *Max Beckmann*. Berlin, 1930.

Wichmann, Hans. *Max Beckmann*. Berlin, 1961.

Wiese, Stephan von. *Max Beckmanns zeichnerisches Werk, 1903-1925*. Düsseldorf, 1978.

Zenser, Hildegard. *Max Beckmann's Selbstbilnisse*. Munich, 1984.

Portfolios and Illustrated Books (Arranged chronologically)

1   Guthmann, Johannes. Euridikes Wiederkehr. Neun Lithographien von Max Beckmann zu den gleichnamigen Versen von Johannes Guthmann. Berlin, Paul Cassirer, 1909. 78 p. plus 9 pl. Limited edition of 60 copies.

2   Beckmann, Max. Sechs Lithographien zum neuen Testament. Berlin, Tieffenbach, 1911.

3   Dostojewski, F. M. Aus einem Totenhaus. Das Bad det Sträflinge. Neun Lithographien von Max Beckmann. Berlin, Cassirer, 1913. Seven of the lithographs in *Kunst und Künstler* II:289-296 1913.

4   Edschmid, Kasimir. Die Fürstin. Mit sechs Radierungen von Max Beckmann. Weimar, Kiepenheuer, 1918. 81 p. plus 6 pl. Limited edition of 500 copies.

5   Beckmann, Max. Gesichter. Original-Radierungen. Einleitung von J. Meier-Graefe. München, Verlag der Marées-Gesellschaft, Piper & Co., 1919. 9 p. plus 19 pl. (Drucke der Marées-Gesellschaft. 13.) Limited edition of 100 copies. Introduction reprinted in Blick auf Beckmann, p. 50-56.

6　Beckmann, Max. Die Hölle. Zehn Originallithographien. Berlin, Graphisches Kabinett, J. B. Neumann, 1919. Limited edition of 75 copies. – Also published in small facsimile edition of 1000 copies.

7　Braunbehrens, Lili von. Stadtnacht. Sieben Lithographien von Max Beckmann zu Gedichten von Lili von Braunbehrens. Munich, Piper, 1921. 47 p. plus 7 pl. Limited edition of 500 copies. – Also published in portfolio in a de luxe edition of 100 copies.

8　Beckmann, Max. Der Jahrmarkt. 10 Original-Radierungen. Munich, Verlag der Marées-Gesellschaft, Piper & Co., 1922. [12] p. plus 10 pl. (Drucke der Marées-Gesellschaft. 36.) Limited edition of 200 copies.

9　Beckmann, Max. Berliner Reise. Zehn Lithographien mit Umschlag und Titelblatt von Max Beckmann. Berlin, J.B. Neumann, 1922. Limited edition of 100 copies.

10　Brentano, Clemens von. Das Märchen von Fanferlieschen Schönefüsschen. Acht Radierungen von Max Beckmann zu dem Märchen von Clemens von Brentano. Berlin, F. Gurlitt, 1924. Limited edition of 220 copies.

11　Beckmann, Max, Ebbi. Komödie. Wien, Johannes-Presse. 1924. 46 p. plus 6 pl. Contains 6 original etchings by the author. Limited edition of 33 copies.

12　Lackner, Stephan. *Der Mensch ist kein Haustier.* Drama. Mit sieben Originallithographien von Max Beckmann. Paris, Editions Cosmopolites, c 1937. 111 p. plus 7 pl. Also in limited edition of 120 numbered and signed copies.

13　Beckmann, Max. Die Apokalypse. Siebenundzwanzig kolorierte Lithographien. Frankfurt am Main, Bauersche Giesserei, 1943.

14　Beckmann, Max. Day & Dream. XV lithographs. N.Y., Curt Valentin, 1946. [4] p. plus 15 pl. Limited edition of 100 copies. – Each lithograph is numbered and signed by the artist.

15　Goethe, Johann Wolfgang von. Faust: der Tragödie zweiter Teil. Mit Bildern von Max Beckmann. [Frankfurt am Main, Bauersche Giesserei, 1957.] 408 p., 2 l. incl. ill. Edition of 850 copies printed for members of the Maximilian Gesellschaft in Hamburg. – The drawings were made by Beckmann 1943-44.

Writings, Statements and Speeches (Arranged chronologically)

1　"Im Kampf um die Kunst (Die Antwort auf den Protest deuscher Künstler)." Munich, Piper Verlag, 1911.

2　"Über den Wert der Kritik." In *Der Angriff* 2 (1912), p. 132.

3　"Gedanken über zeitgemässe Kunst." In *Pan* 2 (March 1912) pp. 499-502.

4　"Das neue Programm" In *Kunst und Künstler* 12:301 incl. ill. 1914.

5   Feldpostbriefe aus dem Westen. [Mit Zeichnungen.] Zusammengestellt von Frau Beckmann-Tube. *Kunst und Künstler* 13:461-467 incl. ill. 1915.

6   Briefe im Kriege. Gesammelt von Minna Tube. Berlin, Cassirer, 1916. 75 p. incl. 17 ill.

7   [Foreword]. *In* Neumann, J. B., Graphisches Kabinett, Berlin. Max Beckmann: Graphik, 1917.

8   Schöpferische Konfession. Herausgegehen von Kasimir Edschmid. 2. Aufl. Berlin, Reiss, 1920. p. 61-67. (Tribüne der Kunst und Zeit. 13.) English translation by Victor H. Meisel in *Voices of Expressionism*, ed. by Meisel, Englewood Cliffs, N.J., 1970.

9   *Das Hotel*, play in four acts, 1912, typescript.

10   *Ebbi*, Komödie, Vienna, 1924.

11   "Autobiographie," *Dem Verlag R. Piper & Co. zum 19 Mai 1924*, p. 10 f.

12   "Der Künstler im Staat," Europäische Revue 3 (1927), p. 287 ff.

13   "Sechs Sentenzen zur Bildgestaltung, in Mannheim, Städtische Kunsthalle, *Max Beckmann: Das gesammelte Werk*, 1928.

14   "Nun sag', wie hast Du's mit der - Politik?" *Frankfurter Zeitung*, Weihnachts-Ausgabe, 1928.

15   "On my Painting," English translation of a lecture entitled "Meine Theorie in der Malerei," given at the New Burlington Galleries, London, July 21, 1938. Cf. Note 1 in "Max Beckmann: Life and Work."

16   *Tagebücher 1940-1950*, Compiled by Mathilde Q. Beckmann, ed. by Erhard Göpel, Munich, 1955; 1959.

17   "Letters to a Woman Painter," translation by Mathilde Q. Beckmann and Perry T. Rathbone of a lecture written in German, but read by Mrs. Beckmann in English at Stephens College, Columbia, MO, Feb, 3, 1948, published in *College Art Journal* 9 (Autumn 1949) 39-43. Reprinted in Peter Selz, *Max Beckmann*, New York, 1964, pp. 132-134.

18   Ansprache für die Freunde und die philosophische Fakultät der Washington University, St. Louis, June 6, 1950. Published in *In memoriam: Max Beckmann*, Frankfurt (Main), 1953, pp. 51-60. English translation in Valentin, Curt, Gallery, New York, *Max Beckmann*, 1954. Translation by Jane Sabersky.

19   "Can Painting Be Taught?" Beckmann's answer (interview) in *Art News* 50 (1951) Nr. 1, pp. 39 ff.

20   "In der Arena der Unendlichkeit," *Die Neue Zeitung*, Munich, February 12, 1952.

21   Twenty letters from 1926-1950, *Briefe an Günther Franke: Portrait*, eines Kunsthändlers, Cologne, 1970.

22   Briefe an Reinhard Piper, in Klaus Gallwitz (ed.) *Max Beckmann*, Frankfurt (Main) 1984.

LIST OF PLATES
(Arranged alphabetically)

The Evening (Self-Portrait with Battenbergs). 1916
Page 33
Courtesy, Alice Adam Ltd., Chicago.

The Family. 1919
Page 36
Courtesy, The Art Institute of Chicago.
Restricted gift of Dr. and Mrs. Martin Gecht,
1989.685.11

The King. 1937
Page 67
Courtesy, The Saint Louis Art Museum.

The Liberated. 1937
Page 69
Courtesy Kuhn & Ehrengkyber, Neusass.

The Night. 1918-1919
Page 31
Courtesy, VG-Bildkunst, Bonn.

The Smoker. 1916
Page 25
Courtesy, Städtische Galerie im Städelschen
Kunstinstut, Frankfurt.

The Way Home. 1919
Page 40
Courtesy, The Art Institute of Chicago.
Restricted gift of Dr. and Mrs. Martin Gecht,
1989.685.2.

Self-Portrait. 1946

Pen and ink, 12¾ x 5¾" (32.5 x 14.5 cm)

Collection, Marianne Feilchenfeldt.